# FAMOUS MOVIE MONSTERS™

# INTRODUCING

# INVASION OF THE BODY SNATCHERS

The Rosen Publishing Group, Inc.,
New York

**KERRY HINTON**

Published in 2007 by The Rosen Publishing Group, Inc.
29 East 21st Street, New York, NY 10010

First Edition

**Library of Congress Cataloging-in-Publication Data**

Hinton, Kerry.
Introducing Invasion of the body snatchers/Kerry Hinton.—1st ed.
   p. cm.—(Famous movie monsters)
Filmography: p.
Includes bibliographical references and index.
ISBN 1-4042-0850-X (library binding)
1. Invasion of the body snatchers (Motion picture: 1956)
I. Title: Invasion of the body snatchers. II. Title. III. Series.

PN1997.I519H56 2006
791.43'72—dc22

                                      2005031282

*Manufactured in Malaysia*

**On the Cover:** Elizabeth Driscoll (Brooke Adams) sleeps as aliens prepare to take over her body in the 1978 remake of *Invasion of the Body Snatchers*.

# CONTENTS

## CHAPTER 1

# INVASION OF THE BODY SNATCHERS

A psychiatrist has been summoned to the emergency room of a city hospital to examine a patient. The patient, Dr. Miles Bennell, is not in the best frame of mind—in fact, he is completely frantic. His suit is covered in mud, his hair is a mess, and two policemen are physically restraining him.

"I'm not crazy!" he shouts. "I'm a doctor, just like you!"

The psychiatrist attempts to calm Miles down and asks him to explain himself. Miles relaxes and begins to tell his story.

Dr. Miles Bennell's tale begins with his return from a medical convention to the sleepy town of Santa Mira, California. His nurse, Sally, informs him that his office was flooded with phone calls and visits from patients while he was out of town. Sally says that the patients refused to see any other doctor in town. Miles notes that this is strange but doesn't dwell on it. Sally also mentions that Miles's former girlfriend,

Becky Driscoll, has returned from England and was one of the people who stopped by.

On their way into town, Miles and Sally almost hit young Jimmy Grimaldi with Miles's car. Jimmy, whose parents run a successful fruit and vegetable business, was running in a panic away from his mother. Mrs. Grimaldi tells Miles that Jimmy is fine—he simply doesn't want to go to school. She also says that the business has become too much work to run and that they have decided to close it down. Again, Miles thinks this is odd, especially since the Grimaldis' business has always been filled with customers.

When Miles returns to his office to see patients, many of them have canceled their appointments. Shortly before lunch, Becky Driscoll arrives at the office and asks Miles to speak to her cousin Wilma. Becky tells Miles that Wilma is suffering from some sort of delusion and is convinced that her uncle Ira is not her uncle Ira. Miles suggests that Becky ask Wilma to make an appointment to see him.

On their way out of the office, Miles and Becky see Police Officer Sam Janzek, who missed his scheduled appointment that day. Miles asks Janzek why he needed medical attention, and Janzek replies, "It wasn't important."

Later that afternoon, Miles has a second encounter with little Jimmy Grimaldi. This time, Jimmy is even more hysterical than he was earlier in the day. His grandmother explains that Jimmy is convinced that his mother is not who she says she is.

Miles goes to see Becky's cousin Wilma and her uncle Ira. When Miles arrives, Becky is with Wilma. Miles speaks with Ira and reports to Wilma that he seems to be the same man she has known her entire life. Wilma agrees that her uncle looks the same and has the same speech and memories, but he acts with no emotion or feeling.

Miles invites Becky to dinner that evening. On their way into the restaurant, they spot Dr. Pursey, the town pediatrician, and Dr. Dan Kauffman, Santa Mira's most respected psychiatrist. Miles asks Dr. Kauffman if he can schedule an appointment for Wilma the next day. Kauffman guesses that Wilma may suspect that someone close to her is not who he or she claims to be. Dr. Pursey mentions that he has referred a dozen patients to Dr. Kauffman for the same condition. Dr. Kauffman tells Miles that he believes that many of the residents of Santa Mira are suffering from mass hysteria. He also says that, in the past two weeks, the hysteria has spread throughout town. Before he drives off, Dr. Kauffman agrees to see Wilma the next afternoon.

Miles and Becky enter the restaurant and find it empty. The owner tells them that he has had very few customers over the past two or three weeks. Before Miles and Becky can sit to have dinner, Miles's nurse, Sally, calls and reports an emergency at the home of Jack Belicec and his wife, Teddy. Becky and Miles leave the restaurant and head for the Belicecs.

At the Belicec home, Jack and his wife act very mysteriously. Jack asks Miles if he can forget he's a doctor and not call the police when he shows him what is inside his house. In the Belicec living room, Jack shows Miles what appears to be a man's corpse. Upon examining the body, Miles and Jack notice that even though the body seems to be that of an adult, the face is very vague and unformed.

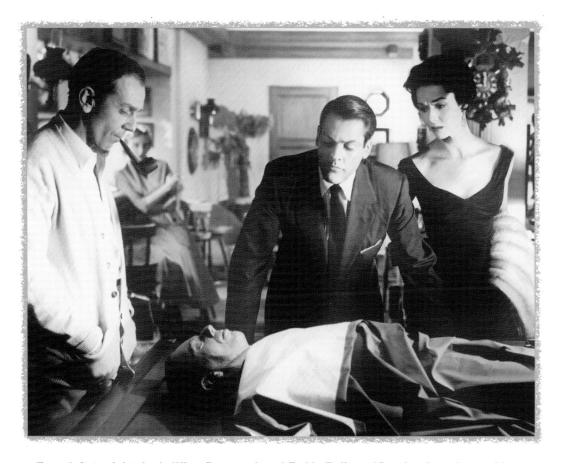

*From left to right:* Jack (King Donovan) and Teddy Belicec (Carolyn Jones) stand by as Dr. Miles Bennell (Kevin McCarthy) and Becky Driscoll (Dana Wynter) examine the strange body found at the Belicecs' house. Teddy suggests that the body is the approximate size and height of her husband. The actress who played Teddy Belicec, Carolyn Jones, is most famous for her role as Morticia Addams in the television series *The Addams Family*.

Miles discovers that the corpse has no fingerprints. Teddy observes that the body is the same height and weight as Jack. Jack is so shocked, he breaks the glass he has in his hand. Miles treats the wound and asks Jack and Teddy to watch the corpse overnight for any changes.

Later that night, Jack and Teddy fall asleep while watching the body. Teddy wakes up and sees that the body is now alive. It has developed facial features identical to those of her husband. Teddy also notices that the body has a cut on his hand in the same place where Jack cut his. Fearing for her life, Teddy awakens Jack and they quickly leave.

Jack and Teddy go to Miles's home and tell him what has happened. Miles calls Dr. Kauffman and asks him to come over. While he is waiting, Miles suddenly develops a strong sense that Becky is in danger. He rushes to the Driscoll house, which is eerily quiet. Miles is sure that something is wrong and takes a trip into the basement. In the cellar, he discovers a body that is forming into an exact replica of Becky. Panicked, Miles finds Becky sleeping and takes her out of the house.

When Miles and Becky return to his house, they find that Teddy and Jack have been joined by Dr. Kauffman. Miles tells the group what he saw in Becky's basement, but Dr. Kauffman doesn't believe the story. Miles, Jack, and Dr. Kauffman go to the Belicec house to investigate. Once there, they discover that Jack's double has disappeared.

Dr. Kauffman sees a blood spot on the pool table and insists that the body was that of a murdered man. He still refuses to accept that the body was not human.

Dr. Kauffman accompanies Jack and Miles to Becky's home, where they find that Becky's replica body is no longer in the basement. Dr. Kauffman still insists that Jack and Miles are victims of mass hysteria. Becky's father, Mr. Driscoll, comes down to the basement, thinking his house is being robbed. By this time the police have arrived and inform everyone that the vanished body turned up in a burning haystack on a local farm. Miles and Jack leave, doubting what they have seen.

The following morning, Miles, Becky, and the Belicecs are still feeling nervous. Jack, Teddy, and Becky all decide to stay at Miles's house. Later, Miles sees Becky's cousin Wilma. Wilma asks him to cancel her appointment with Dr. Kauffman, saying that she feels fine.

At the office, Miles sees Jimmy Grimaldi with his mother. Jimmy is no longer afraid of her and seems completely recovered. Something seems wrong to Miles, and his suspicions continue to grow.

That night, Miles and Becky get together with the Belicecs for dinner. Everything seems normal until Miles goes into the greenhouse in his backyard. Once inside, he sees a disturbing sight—objects that look like large pea pods are opening to reveal still-forming bodies. Miles thinks about the bodies in Becky's basement and Jack's house and realizes that the pods are producing duplicate bodies. These "pod people" take over the lives of their victims while they are sleeping.

Miles tries to call for help, but the operator tells him that all numbers outside of Santa Mira are busy. Suspicious, Miles believes that a large part of the town must have been replaced by pod people. Jack and Teddy leave to get help outside of Santa Mira, while Miles and Becky remain behind. Miles destroys the pods with a pitchfork and leaves with Becky.

Miles decides to call his nurse, Sally, hoping she is still unaffected. At the gas station, Miles tries the phone, but there is no answer. As he waits, he sees the station attendant looking in the trunk of his car. Down the road, Miles stops the car

and finds the trunk full of pods. He removes them and burns them in the street.

Many cars are parked outside Sally's house. Miles leaves Becky in the car and sneaks around back to investigate. Peering through a window, he sees that a group of pod people is gathered inside the house. Miles watches with horror as Becky's father enters the room with a pod and asks Sally if her baby is asleep yet.

"Not yet, but she will be soon," says Sally. "And then there will be no more tears."

While Miles looks on, Officer Janzek approaches from behind to capture him.

"Why don't you go in, Miles? We've been waiting for you," he says.

Miles manages to escape Officer Janzek, but the police put out an all points bulletin on Miles and Becky to prevent their escape from town. Every police car in Santa Mira patrols the town in search of them. Miles and Becky abandon their car and hide in Miles's office, where Miles gives her pills to help her stay awake.

Miles and Becky manage not to fall asleep. In the morning, they see the townspeople going about their everyday business. A bus pulls up and lets off passengers Miles has never seen before.

Miles and Becky run for their lives from the pod people of sleepy Santa Mira. To escape, they leave the populated town and head for the surrounding hills. This scene was shot in the small town of Sierra Madre, California, which was also used as a setting for other famous horror films, such as John Carpenter's *Halloween* (1978) and *The Fog* (1980).

A few minutes later, a siren sounds, and everyone outside gathers in the town square. Three trucks filled with pods arrive, and the townspeople line up to receive one each. Suddenly, it all becomes clear to Miles—farmers are growing pods and distributing them throughout town, possibly to the entire world.

Jack arrives, revealing that he and Teddy have become pod people. He tells Miles and Becky that they are the only normal people left in town. Some men enter the room with pods meant to replace Miles and Becky.

"Would you like to watch them grow?" Dr. Kauffman asks. "Sooner or later you'll have to go to sleep."

He also tells Miles and Becky how the pods came to be. They were originally seeds drifting through space. Now that they have landed on Earth, they are able to reproduce themselves in any form of life. Dr. Kauffman says that the pods will absorb the minds and memories of their victims, but the world will be reborn as one with no pain, desire, ambition, or faith.

Miles tells Dr. Kauffman and Jack that he wants no part of that world.

"You have no choice!" says Dr. Kauffman. He and Jack leave, locking Miles and Becky inside with the pods.

Once Dr. Kauffman and Jack leave, Miles fills three syringes with a sedative and creates a distraction. When Jack and Dr. Kauffman enter the room, he injects them. After they fall unconscious, Miles and Becky escape.

As they leave the office, Miles tells Becky that to survive, they must act as if they are pod people themselves, showing no interest or excitement.

Outside, they see Officer Janzek and tell him they have been replaced. He seems to believe them. As they walk away, a dog runs in front of a bus, causing Becky to shriek, "Watch out!" Officer Janzek becomes suspicious and activates the main siren.

Miles and Becky run for their lives through the woods and into the hills surrounding Santa Mira, with much of the town in pursuit. Becky begins to grow increasingly sleepy as they run, so Miles carries her.

Exhausted, they hide under a walkway inside a cave. Miles hears beautiful music in the distance. He thinks that since music is filled with emotion, there may still be some normal people left in town.

When Miles goes outside, however, he sees that the music is coming from a radio in the valley below where people are filling trucks with thousands of pods. Returning to the cave, he finds that Becky has become a pod person. In the short time since he's been away, her body and mind have been taken over. Becky alerts the other pod people to Miles's location. They chase him to the highway, where he tries to warn the people driving to get help and to stay away from the town. The pod people do not follow Miles, believing that people outside of Santa Mira will think he is insane.

"Stop and listen to me!" Miles calls to the passing vehicles. "They aren't human!"

None of the drivers on the highway believe Miles. He hops on a passing truck to ride out of town and sees that it is carrying thousands of pods bound for San Francisco and

In one of the film's most famous scenes, Miles tries in vain to warn anyone he can of the danger spreading outward from Santa Mira. Actor Kevin McCarthy appeared in a number of films after *Invasion of the Body Snatchers*, including the classic 1981 were-wolf movie *The Howling*.

Los Angeles. He jumps down to the street in horror and tries to alert passersby.

"You fools! They're here already!"

None of the cars and trucks stop as Miles continues his warning.

"You're next!" he screams. "You're next!"

Finished with his story, Miles is shocked to find that the doctors don't believe him. They are preparing to take him to the mental hospital when a man is wheeled into the emergency room. The ambulance driver tells the doctors that the patient's truck collided with a bus and was overturned. He also mentions that the driver had to be dug out of a pile of strange pods that had come from Santa Mira.

It seems that Miles's story just may be true. The doctors call the police and tell them to block all highways and stop all traffic. As the psychiatrist from the state hospital orders someone to call the FBI, Miles falls against the wall, exhausted yet relieved that help is on the way.

## CHAPTER 2

# HISTORY OF AN INVASION

*Invasion of the Body Snatchers* was based on a book by Jack Finney simply entitled *Body Snatchers*. *Body Snatchers* was originally serialized in *Collier's* magazine. Popular with fans of science fiction and horror, it was released as a paperback in 1955.

One of the book's many fans was a film producer named Walter Wanger, who read the book as each segment was published in *Collier's*. Wanger was familiar with Jack Finney's previous book, *5 Against the House*, which had recently been adapted for the big screen. Upon reading *Body Snatchers*, Wanger gave a copy to director Don Siegel.

Siegel liked the story and thought it would work well as a motion picture. As Siegel says in his autobiography, *A Siegel Film*, he envisioned a movie that could be "not only entertaining, but frightening as well." He hired veteran screenwriter Daniel Mainwaring to write the script. He cast a British actress named Dana Wynter as Becky Driscoll and chose Kevin McCarthy to play

**Don Siegel** *(left)* **and Walter Wanger** *(right)* **on the set of 1954's** *Riot in Cell Block 11*.
**Wanger's experiences as a prison inmate prompted him to make a film about the**
**dehumanizing effects of incarceration and prison life. Wanger and Siegel's next proj-**
**ect,** *Invasion of the Body Snatchers*, **also dealt with what it is like to lose one's**
**individuality.**

Dr. Miles Bennell. McCarthy and Siegel had previously worked
together in *An Annapolis Story* (1955). Siegel liked McCarthy's
acting and thought he'd be perfect to play the male lead.

## B MOVIES

Walter Wanger worked for Allied Artists, a company that had a
reputation for making B movies. B movies were played in theaters

to support higher-budget films with big-name stars. In the 1950s, moviegoers would usually be treated to two movies— the headlining film and the B movie. Since the cost of making these B movies was much lower than feature films, B movies were able to take chances in storytelling and directing that studios were not willing to risk with big-budget movies. B movies also gave directors and actors with less experience a chance to perfect their skills in a real work setting.

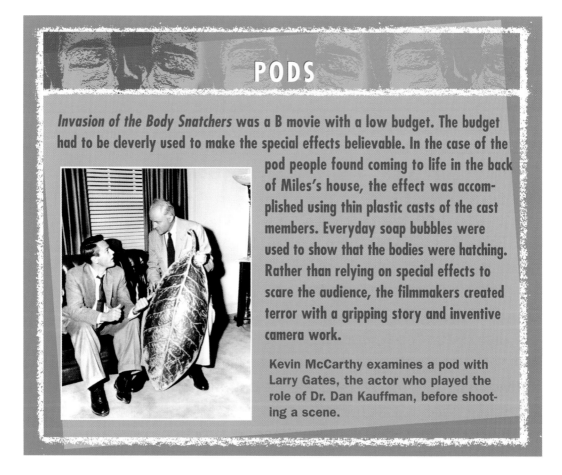

## PODS

*Invasion of the Body Snatchers* was a B movie with a low budget. The budget had to be cleverly used to make the special effects believable. In the case of the pod people found coming to life in the back of Miles's house, the effect was accomplished using thin plastic casts of the cast members. Everyday soap bubbles were used to show that the bodies were hatching. Rather than relying on special effects to scare the audience, the filmmakers created terror with a gripping story and inventive camera work.

Kevin McCarthy examines a pod with Larry Gates, the actor who played the role of Dr. Dan Kauffman, before shooting a scene.

## A PERFECT PARTNERSHIP

Wanger and Siegel's working relationship made *Invasion of the Body Snatchers* more than just a B movie. Walter Wanger, who had spent time in prison, was a proponent of movies dealing with societal problems. Don Siegel had directed the successful film *Riot in Cell Block 11* (1954), a movie about prison reform, for Wanger. Wanger thought that Siegel would do a good job with *Invasion of the Body Snatchers.*

A promotional poster for the movie *Riot in Cell Block 11* (1954). The success of *Riot in Cell Block 11* laid the foundation for producer Walter Wanger and director Don Siegel to work on *Invasion of the Body Snatchers* two years later. Like *Invasion of the Body Snatchers, Riot in Cell Block 11* deals with a small group of characters who are attempting to rebel against horrible and seemingly impossible circumstances.

Both Wanger and Siegel saw more than a simple horror story in Jack Finney's book. To them, *Invasion of the Body Snatchers* also criticized the idea of conformity in American culture. Throughout the rest of his career, Siegel would mention his dislike for "pod people," or men and women who, like the residents of Santa Mira, walked through life with no sense of individuality or emotions. Siegel's experience shooting gritty films like *Riot in Cell Block 11* showed through in *Invasion of the Body Snatchers.* Under Siegel's direction, what could

Actors Kevin McCarthy and Dana Wynter receive direction on the set from Don Siegel. They are rehearsing before shooting the scene in which Miles and Becky hide under a walkway inside an abandoned mine to evade the residents of Santa Mira, who have all been transformed into pod people.

have been a simple, silly science fiction movie became a deadly serious commentary on losing one's individuality.

## ANYTOWN, U.S.A.

*Invasion of the Body Snatchers* was filmed in the small town of Sierra Madre, California. This setting was carefully chosen. Santa Mira was meant to represent any number of communities around the country. The idea that such a normal, all-American town could be completely taken over in a matter of weeks made the story seem even more frightening.

*Invasion of the Body Snatchers* was shot in only nineteen days, and it cost about $300,000 (the equivalent of slightly more than $2 million today). The specially made pods alone cost the studio $30,000 (around $200,000 today). Despite the constraints of a small budget and short timeframe, the dedicated cast and crew managed to turn out an extremely well-made movie.

The shooting schedule meant that there was very little time for the cast to rest on the set. The actors were truly exhausted during some of the chase scenes, making them look extremely realistic. For instance, when Miles is trying to alert the world to the existence of the pod people at the end of the movie, he appears to be frantic and exhausted. Actor Kevin McCarthy was so tired from the relentless shooting schedule that he barely had to act at all.

## THE STUDIO STEPS IN

Allied Artists became very involved in the making of *Invasion of the Body Snatchers*. Since the studio was funding the movie, they were concerned about whether or not it would be a success at the box office. As a result of this concern, they decided to make a number of plot changes that they thought would make it a more popular film. Many of their decisions did not go

### SLEEP NO MORE

An alternate title Kevin McCarthy suggested for *Invasion of the Body Snatchers* was *Sleep No More*. The idea came from a line in the play *Hamlet* by William Shakespeare, and it refers to the gradual "waking up" of Miles as he realizes the aliens have arrived. The phrase also refers to the fact that pod people took over their victim's bodies while they were asleep.

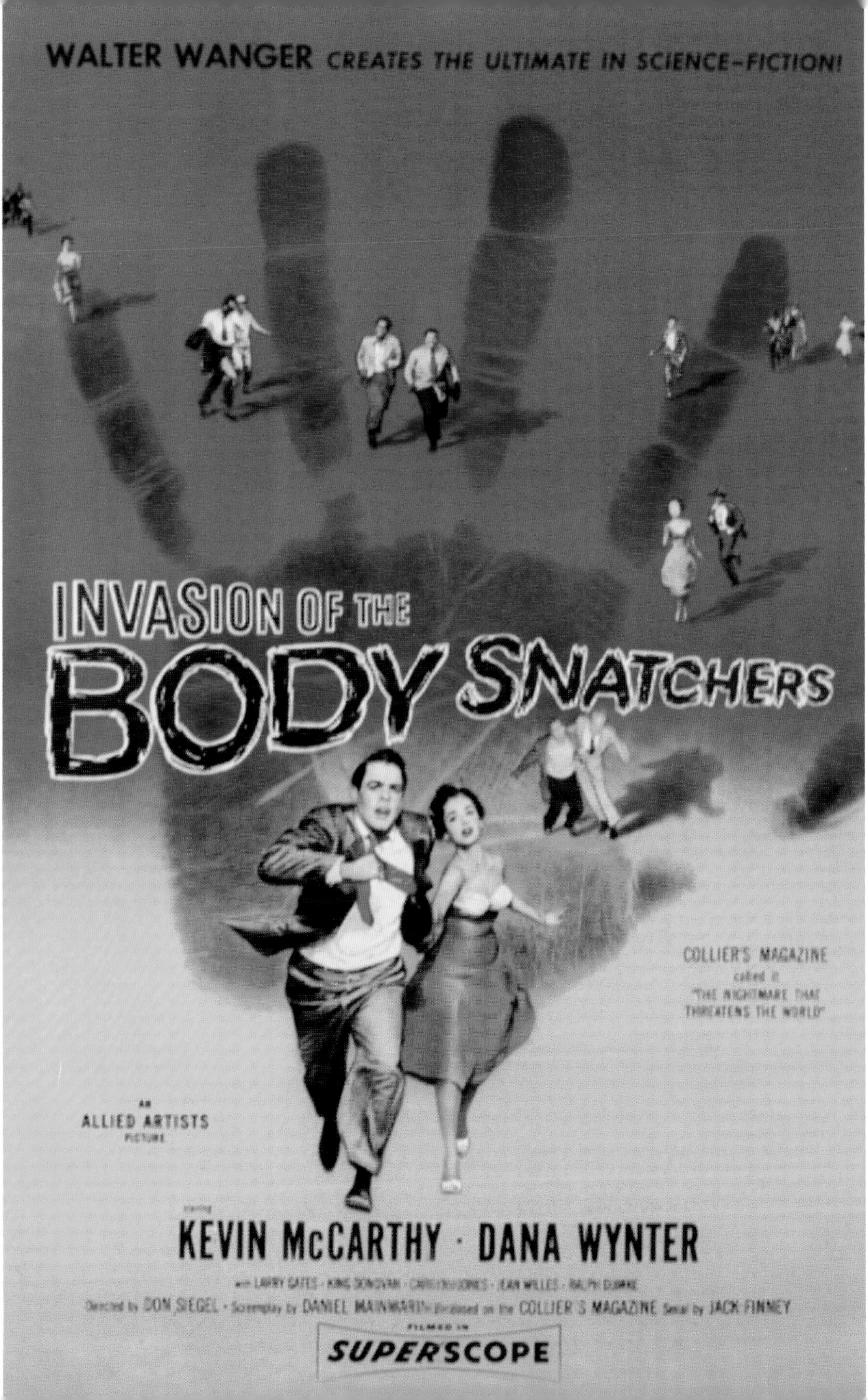
WALTER WANGER CREATES THE ULTIMATE IN SCIENCE-FICTION!
INVASION OF THE
BODY SNATCHERS
COLLIER'S MAGAZINE
called it
"THE NIGHTMARE THAT
THREATENS THE WORLD"
AN
ALLIED ARTISTS
PICTURE
KEVIN McCARTHY · DANA WYNTER
Directed by DON SIEGEL · Screenplay by DANIEL MAINWARING · Based on the COLLIER'S MAGAZINE Serial by JACK FINNEY
FILMED IN
SUPERSCOPE

This original U.S. promotional poster for *Invasion of the Body Snatchers* shows Miles and Becky running from an unseen threat. Despite its small budget, the film was successful in many different countries. The film was further assured a place in history when it was selected to the National Film Registry in the Library of Congress in 1994.

over well with the cast and crew. For instance, Allied Artists insisted that Don Siegel change the name of the movie from *Body Snatchers* (the original title of Jack Finney's book) to *Invasion of the Body Snatchers*. Allied Artists also did away with much of the humor that Mainwaring and Siegel had intended to be in the movie. The original screenplay was funny and scary at the same time, and people were both laughing out loud and screaming in fear at a test screening. Allied Artists wanted to market a straight horror movie, however, and most of the comedy was edited out.

The biggest change occurred, however, with the movie's ending. Don Siegel wanted the movie to end with a close-up of Miles's face screaming, "You're next!" as he asks for help on the highway. Allied Artists considered this ending too bleak and depressing. To soften the ending, they decided to add two scenes to the film. First, a prologue was filmed, allowing Miles to tell his story as a flashback. Doing this let the audience know that the hero was not going to die. Next, an epilogue to the movie was shot in which the authorities finally believe Miles's story, ending the movie on a much more hopeful note.

## CHAPTER 3

# THE ROOTS OF AN INVASION

Unlike many other horror films and monster movies, *Invasion of the Body Snatchers* creates fear without the aid of fantastic-looking creatures or graphic violence. The idea of a monster who is undetectable is the most unsettling aspect of the film. Although the pod people look like normal, everyday human beings, they have lost their individuality, free will, and ability to feel. In short, they have lost their humanity.

## DOPPELGÄNGERS

The idea of a double, or duplicate person, can be traced back to creatures in German mythology called doppelgängers. In German, "doppelgänger" literally means "double goer," or "double walker." Doppelgängers are often described as "shadow selves" that can only be seen by the person whose likeness they have assumed. Generally, doppelgängers were considered to be malevolent creatures. Some myths say that when these doubles do appear, it can result in tragedy or death for the person who sees them. Others portray doppelgängers as mischievous spirits who actively cause trouble for their other halves.

The threat of losing one's identity does not affect just one individual in *Invasion of the Body Snatchers*, but an entire town. If the aliens win, the identity of an entire group of people will vanish.

## BRAINWASHING

Finney's main goal in writing *Body Snatchers* was to entertain people. However, both the book and the movie adaptation echoed aspects of American life that were terrifying in their own ways.

The fear of losing one's identity was common in American society during the 1950s. In the early part of the decade, the United States went to war in Korea following Communist North Korea's invasion of South Korea. The United States entered the conflict on the side of South Korea. At the time, the U.S. government believed that Communism would spread from one country to another if left unchecked. The government felt that it was the duty of the United States to make sure that this did not happen.

When prisoners of war returned from the conflict, there were rumors that they had been brainwashed by their captors to work as undercover Communist agents in the United States. Although these rumors were never proven to be true, many people found the idea that someone could be made to believe in something he or she was fundamentally opposed to both terrifying and fascinating.

# MASS HYSTERIA

In *Invasion of the Body Snatchers*, Jimmy and Wilma claim that people they loved are no longer the same. Dr. Kauffman attributes their odd behavior to an outbreak of mass hysteria. Mass hysteria is a phenomenon that occurs when a large group of people suddenly acquire the same symptoms of an illness or all share the same irrational behavior.

For instance, at a school in Florida in the early 1990s, a child complained that her sandwich tasted funny. Minutes later, she became ill. All of the children in the cafeteria had the same lunch. Within forty minutes, almost half of them had the same symptoms as the first girl. An hour later, no one was sick. When the lunches were tested, they were found to be perfectly safe. Mass hysteria had caused the children to believe that they were sick.

Salem, Massachusetts, was the location of one of the most famous examples of mass hysteria in the United States. Salem was an extremely religious Puritan community. In 1692, Salem's residents became convinced that many men and women in town were witches. By the time people came to their senses, nineteen people had been tried and hanged for practicing witchcraft.

*The Duckingstool* (circa 1870–1896), by Charles Stanley Reinhart, depicts the dunking of a woman in water to determine whether or not she is a witch. The accused was usually bound or made to hold a heavy stone. If the person floated, he or she was considered a witch and often sentenced to death. If the person sank, he or she was declared innocent. Many accused witches found innocent in this manner drowned before they could be rescued.

Soviet soldiers march in Red Square, Moscow, prior to the fall of the Berlin Wall in 1989. Moscow had served as the center of the United Soviet Socialist Republic's (USSR) Communist government since the Russian Revolution of 1917. Many Americans were frightened of Communism and became convinced that it could spread in the United States.

## COMMUNISM

Mistrust of Communism was widespread in the United States. Many Americans saw it as a system that took many personal freedoms away. Theoretically, Communism was supposed to result in all citizens sharing the ownership of land and property.

COMM̲̅ RTY ORGANIZATION U.S.A-FEB. 9, 1950

Senator Joseph McCarthy was the driving force behind a series of congressional hearings during the 1950s to identify supporters of the Communist party in the United States. Many careers were ruined when people in film, television, and academia were blacklisted as a result of McCarthy's hearings.

In practice, Communist ideas often became twisted into a system in which ruthless totalitarian governments attempted to control every detail of their citizens' lives. For the average American citizen, the pod people of *Invasion of the Body Snatchers* seemed like metaphors for Communists.

## McCARTHYISM

In the early 1950s, many members of the United States govern-ment decided to root out Communism at home. The House Un-American Activities Committee (HUAC) was formed to investi-gate the presence of Communists in the U.S. government, entertainment industry, and education system.

Spearheaded by Senator Joseph McCarthy, HUAC falsely accused a great number of people of being Communists. Many people were affected by HUAC's investigations, from people who had once attended Communist meetings to people who had close friends or business partners who were Communists. Many people targeted by HUAC were not Communists at all.

Individuals suspected of being Communists were often jailed or blacklisted. Blacklisting was a practice by which employers would not hire people suspected to be Communists because of their beliefs.

## CONFORMITY

Conformity plays a large part in *Invasion of the Body Snatchers*. In the 1950s, conformity, or fitting in, was generally seen as being very important.

The two decades prior to the 1950s were a difficult time for most Americans. The Great Depression of the 1930s left many in dire poverty, and America's involvement in World War II in the 1940s resulted in many men and women making great sacrifices.

Suburban mothers and their children meet diaper delivery trucks in their neighborhood—a common sight in the 1950s and 1960s. Don Siegel disliked the idea of performing everyday tasks in an endless routine with little thought or creativity. His hatred of conformity would translate into the emotionless pod people of *Invasion of the Body Snatchers*.

After World War II, the U.S. economy began to slowly recover. Materials that had been rationed for the war effort, such as gasoline, were widely available once more. Many Americans wished for nothing but calm and normality after the turmoil of the war. The desire to maintain the status quo, or keep things as they are, sometimes resulted in the neglect of social problems such as poverty and segregation that were still widespread in the United States. Sometimes, people who spoke out against these problems were accused of being un-American. Many Americans at the time didn't want to stick out or appear to be different from what was considered to be normal.

Critics of conformity complained that this way of life robbed people of individual thoughts and actions. Many people saw *Invasion of the Body Snatchers* as an anticonformity movie that related to the "pod people" of everyday life. In the film, for example, Dr. Kauffman and Jack Belicec urge Miles and Becky to be like them, but they refuse to conform. They decide that they would rather be themselves, flaws and everything.

## CHAPTER 4

# THE LEGACY OF THE POD PEOPLE

*Invasion of the Body Snatchers* became a popular film that developed a large cult following, but no one is a bigger fan of it than Kevin McCarthy himself. In an August 3, 2000, interview with the *Provincetown Bee*, McCarthy said, "*Invasion of the Body Snatchers* is the most outstanding sci-fi picture ever made. I made it in 1955 and every day of my life it's still operative. There are always letters in the mailbox, fans call me, e-mail me, and it all has to do with a fairly modest movie."

Although the star of a movie may be biased toward his or her work in a film, there is no disputing the fact that *Invasion of the Body Snatchers* is as loved today as it was when it was released in 1956. *Time* magazine named it one of the top 100 movies of all time. In 1994, the National Film Preservation Board chose *Invasion of the Body Snatchers* to be preserved in the Library of Congress as part of the National Film Registry, insuring the film's place in cinema history.

# KEVIN McCARTHY: TWO INVASIONS

The influence of *Invasion of the Body Snatchers* has been so great since its release in 1956 that many of its remakes have been very faithful to the ideas of the original movie. Philip Kaufman took this one step further by casting the star of the 1956 film in his 1978 remake. Kevin McCarthy, who played Dr. Miles Bennell, made a cameo as a seemingly insane man screaming at traffic in downtown San Francisco, California. Kaufman even chose to give McCarthy some of the dialogue he spoke twenty-two years earlier. As McCarthy screams,

"They're already here!" viewers are cleverly reminded of the original version.

In the 1978 remake of *Invasion of the Body Snatchers*, Kevin McCarthy, in a small guest role, attempts to warn Matthew Bennell (Donald Sutherland) of the dangerous nature of the beautiful yet deadly flowers blooming in metropolitan San Francisco. Director Philip Kaufman also cast Don Siegel and himself in small cameo roles.

*Invasion of the Body Snatchers* was not a huge success at first. At the time, science fiction movies were usually regarded as entertainment for children. People began taking the film more seriously, however, after European film critics praised its artistic merits. It was clear to them that *Invasion of the Body Snatchers* was no ordinary horror film. Don Siegel used many techniques associated with film noir, a style of filmmaking that

Pursued by the townspeople, Miles and Becky hide in an abandoned mine. The actual cave was one of the Bronson Caves of Griffith Park, Los Angeles. This cave is known by many locals as the "bat cave" since it was used on the television series *Batman*, which ran from 1966 to 1968. Siegel's heavy use of shadows and contrast in scenes like this has often been compared to film noir.

used high-contrast black-and-white film, dramatic camera angles, and unusual lighting to create a disturbing atmosphere. Siegel's direction made the most normal settings seem claustrophobic and eerie. European critics understood and appreciated Siegel's attention to detail, and eventually American critics did as well.

Word of mouth also helped the movie's success. Many people who saw it told their friends about the curious and terrifying new horror movie. *Invasion of the Body Snatchers* may not have been a blockbuster upon its release, but the praise it received in the United States and abroad made it a very profitable movie, especially considering its low budget.

## ALL TYPES OF SUCCESS

No one had any idea that a small B movie with a strange title would affect so many people across the globe. Throughout Europe, the movie was shown without the prologue and epilogue, finally giving life to the original vision of Don Siegel and Walter Wanger. Later screenings in America did the same, but the DVD and VHS versions available today in the United States have the more positive ending.

Invasion of the Body Snatchers became even more popular and successful once Allied Artists allowed television stations to play the film. Most stations showed it as a late-night feature, making it available to a new generation of horror fans.

## REALITY CAN BE TERRIFYING

Setting a film in a familiar environment gives it an added dose of realism, even if the danger or threat is alien or supernatural. The effectiveness of *Invasion of the Body Snatchers* lies in its simple, small-town setting. Don Siegel realized that many things are frightening, but they are even more so when they happen to be next door. Although partly a cost-saving measure, the lack

In *The Stepford Wives* (1975), directed by Bryan Forbes, the men of a small suburban community gradually replace their wives with animatronic robots. This comic
and chilling film was one of the highest-grossing films of the seventies. *The Stepford
Wives* deals with similar concepts that *Invasion of the Body Snatchers* does, particularly what it means to lose one's individuality.

of special effects in *Invasion of the Body Snatchers* created a
new kind of horror movie. Rather than relying on fantastic creatures to frighten audiences, *Invasion of the Body Snatchers*
uses paranoia.

Although not directly inspired by *Invasion of the Body
Snatchers*, there have been many movies since 1956 that have

tackled the idea of close friends and loved ones changing into something else, including *The Stepford Wives* (1975) and John Carpenter's *The Thing* (1982).

In *The Stepford Wives*, a woman named Joanna Eberhart moves to a small town in Connecticut where everything seems normal. Although her husband enjoys the town, Joanna thinks that something is wrong. All of the women who live there seem strange. It isn't long before she discovers that the men in the town have killed their wives and replaced them with robots.

In *The Thing*, a group of scientists on an Antarctic research expedition comes across a shape-shifting alien life-form. The alien has the ability to assume the form of its victims, and soon the scientists can't tell who has been taken over by the alien and who hasn't.

## OTHER INVASIONS

*Invasion of the Body Snatchers* has proven to be more influential and popular than its creators could have imagined. Since 1956, there have been two remakes of *Invasion of the Body Snatchers*. The first remake, also entitled *Invasion of the Body Snatchers*, premiered in 1978. Kevin McCarthy had a small role in the film, which featured the actors Donald Sutherland, Leonard Nimoy, Jeff Goldblum, and Brooke Adams. Director Philip Kaufman raises the stakes by setting the action in the modern-day metropolis of San Francisco. This choice of setting is particularly interesting, as San Francisco was one of the focal points of social awareness in the 1960s. If pod people can take over such a diverse and unique city, what hope does the rest of society have?

The origin of the pod people is explained during the opening credits, as the viewer is treated to a vision of alien spores floating through space toward Earth. The spores attach themselves to local plants and produce beautiful if strange flowers. These flowers eventually grow to become large pods capable of taking over people's bodies while they sleep. The aliens in this version of the story use chilling, high-pitched screams to notify each other of unchanged humans in the area. By the time that scream is heard, it is usually too late to escape.

The basic elements of Siegel's 1956 film are in place, but Kaufman manages to make the movie his own. Philip Kaufman's film includes much more humor than Siegel's, and it ends on a much more sinister note. It also relies on many more special effects than the original. In 1979, the Academy of Science Fiction, Fantasy and Horror Films awarded Philip Kaufman the Saturn Award for Best Director.

A 1993 remake simply entitled *Body Snatchers* strays further from the original version. Director Abel Ferrara moves the setting to a military base and loads the film with special effects. As in the previous films, people don't seem to be themselves. Unlike the previous films, outside authorities are aware of the problem. They send a scientist from the Environmental Protection Agency, who suspects the strange behavior may be due to a toxic spill in the area. As the movie progresses, the scientist learns that the real explanation may lie in the strange pods that have been found in a local lake.

Although both versions did well in theaters, neither has been able to match the original in the eyes of many fans. The legacy of the film lives on today as well. In 2006, Nicole Kidman is set to

Matthew Bennell (Donald Sutherland) sleeps in the 1978 version of *Invasion of the Body Snatchers.* As he sleeps, he is surrounded by pods that begin to hatch. Bennell manages to destroy the pods with a gardening implement and escape.

star in the fourth movie based on Jack Finney's chilling tale. Although each of the remakes is different, they all share one thing in common: the hero of each movie becomes isolated from the rest of society and does not know who can be trusted and who cannot.

For such a small film, *Invasion of the Body Snatchers* has proven to be more influential and popular than its creators could have imagined. The fact that such a tight shooting schedule and small budget resulted in an excellent film still influences many directors in the present day. Many independent films are now being made with budgets comparable to *Invasion of the Body Snatchers* and tackle issues and ideas that larger blockbuster films may not address.

Generation after generation has had the pleasure of being scared by the unique vision of Jack Finney and Don Siegel. The themes of resisting conformity and losing one's identity in *Invasion of the Body Snatchers* are timeless, and they will terrify moviegoers for years to come.

# FILMOGRAPHY

*Invasion of the Body Snatchers* (1956). The original Don Siegel film, starring Kevin McCarthy and Dana Wynter, still sets the standard for paranoid horror films.

*The Stepford Wives* (1975). A movie that deals with similar themes of conformity as *Invasion of the Body Snatchers*. In this case, women are being replaced with obedient robots by their husbands.

*Invasion of the Body Snatchers* (1978). The first remake by director Philip Kaufman relies on many more special effects than the original film, but it is still very effective. Kaufman places the action in the metropolis of San Francisco, California. Doing this allowed him to expand on the small-town dynamics of the original movie, as the aliens are shown taking over an entire city. Starring Donald Sutherland, Brooke Adams, Jeff Goldblum, and Leonard Nimoy, this version of the film shows the outer space origin of the pods during the opening credits.

John Carpenter's *The Thing* (1982). This remake of the 1951 horror movie *The Thing from Another World* is only loosely based on the plot of the original. In this version, a group of scientists conducting research in Antarctica encounters an alien that can assume the shape and thoughts of its victims. Although this movie borrows heavily from elements of *Invasion of the Body Snatchers*, it has a vastly different plot.

*Body Snatchers* (1993) Directed by Abel Ferrara, this remake of the horror classic is set on an air force base. In this version of the film, the pods are initially thought to be the result of pollution before they are discovered to be from outer space.

# GLOSSARY

**biased**  Prejudiced against someone or something.

**B movie**  A low-budget movie that was usually played with a main feature in theaters.

**Communism**  A system of government in which social classes and private property are abolished.

**conformity**  Adherence to a set of social standards without question.

**corpse**  A dead body.

**dehumanization**  The taking away of human qualities, such as individuality.

**elude**  To escape.

**epilogue**  A short addition at the end of a book or film.

**film noir**  A type of film that often features dramatic lighting, a bleak setting, and corrupt characters.

**individuality**  The qualities that make one person different from another.

**mass hysteria**  A condition in which a large group of people exhibit similar hysterical physical or emotional symptoms.

**producer**  A person who finds financing for and supervises the making of a play or film.

**prologue**  A short addition at the beginning of a book or film.

**replica**  A copy or reproduction.

**sedative**  A drug that can soothe or calm. In larger doses, sedatives can cause sleep or death.

# FOR MORE INFORMATION

Hollywood History Museum
1660 North Highland Avenue
Hollywood, CA 90028
(323) 464-7776
Web site: http://www.thehollywoodmuseum.com

The Museum of Television and Radio
25 West 52nd Street
New York, NY 10019
(212) 621-6800
Web site: http://www.mtr.org

Science Fiction Museum and Hall of Fame
325 5th Avenue South
Seattle, WA 98109
(206) 724-3428
Web site: http://www.sfhomeworld.org

## WEB SITES

Due to the changing nature of Internet links, the Rosen Publishing Group, Inc., has developed an online list of Web sites related to the subject of this book. The site is updated regularly. Please use this link to access the list:

http://www.rosenlinks.com/famm/inbs

# FOR FURTHER READING

Finney, Jack. *Invasion of the Body Snatchers*. New York, NY: Touchstone, 1995.

Levin, Ira. *The Stepford Wives*. New York, NY: Harper Paperbacks, 2002.

McCarthy, Kevin, and Edward Gorman, eds. *"They're Here..."*: Invasion of the Body Snatchers: *A Tribute.* New York, NY: Berkley Publishing Group, 1999.

Skal, David J. *The Monster Show: A Cultural History of Horror*. London, England: Faber & Faber, 2001.

Sterling, Robert, ed. *The Book of Doppelgangers*. Rockville, MD: Wildside Press, 2003.

# BIBLIOGRAPHY

"*Film Notes:* Invasion of the Body Snatchers." New York State Writers' Institute, State University of New York. Retrieved July 1, 2005 (http://www.albany.edu/writers-inst/fnf03n6.html).

Finney, Jack. *Invasion of the Body Snatchers*. New York, NY: Touchstone, 1995.

"*Greatest Films:* Invasion of the Body Snatchers." Filmsite.org. Retrieved July 1, 2005 (http://filmsite.org/inva.html).

"*Invasion of the Body Snatchers*." The Science Fiction, Horror and Fantasy Film Review. Retrieved July 15, 2005 (http://www.moria.co.nz/sf/bodysnatchers56.htm).

"*Invasion of the Body Snatchers*." Shotgun Reviews. Retrieved July 15, 2005 (http://www.shotgunreviews.com/reviews/columns/barker2.html).

McCarthy, Kevin, ed. *"They're Here . . . ":* Invasion of the Body Snatchers: *A Tribute*. New York, NY: Berkley Publishing Group, 1999.

# INDEX

## ABOUT THE AUTHOR

Kerry Hinton is a writer who lives and works in Hoboken, New Jersey. *Invasion on the Body Snatchers* first scared him in 1978, and continues to do so today. This is his fifth book for the Rosen Publishing Group.

## PHOTO CREDITS

Cover, pp. 1, 14, 19, 33, 34 © Photofest; pp. 4, 7, 10, 16, 17, 18, 20, 22, 24, 32, 36, 39 © Everett Collection; pp. 26, 27 © Bettmann/Corbis; p. 28 © Getty Images; p. 30 © Ralph Crane/Time & Life Pictures/Getty Images.

Design: Thomas Forget